I0560459

From Silence to SoulFire:

A Mother's Truth. A Soul's Legacy

Tamara Scott

First Edition

ISBN: 979-8-9928622-7-0

Publisher: Rise2Write Publishing LLC

www.rise2write.com

Cover design by Tamara Scott

Interior design by Tamara Scott

Printed in the United States of America

10 9 8 7 6 5 4 3 2 1

This is a work of nonfiction. Names, characters, places, and incidents are either the product of the author's experiences and recollections or are used fictitiously. Any resemblance to actual people, living or dead, is purely coincidental unless otherwise stated.

I dedicate this book to my children, Ilasia, Jaylun, Jy'Miere, Iymoni, Issiah Jr, and Izreal, for going through the fire with me. My mother, Lorraine, and big brother, Emery Sr, for always having my back in any situation. My husband James, for supporting me throughout this journey. It was rough and your love, loyalty, and support never wavered and to Envista Credit Union for all the free ink pens I went through for my manuscript.

This book is a vessel of healing, truth, and emotional depth. It's not just a memoir-it's an offering of compassion, understanding, and spiritual medicine. Sharing my truth with softness, not shame, with grace, not guilt. My emotional wisdom is distilled into words that will guide my daughters- and other women too. My story is sacred, my voice is powerful, and each word I write is a thread in the tapestry of healing.

Prologue

Before I was the woman you know-before the love, before the wisdom, before the rising. I was a girl trying to make sense of a world that didn't make space for her softness. I've carried many names, many roles, daughter, mother, wife, survivor. But long before I learned to own any of them, I learned how to disappear in plain sight. I learned how to smile through the pain, how to protect my heart with silence and how to keep giving even when I had nothing left for myself.

This book is not just a retelling of my past. It's a reckoning. A reclaiming. A remembering of the woman I buried beneath expectations, heartbreak, and survival. It's a love letter to the girl I once was and to the daughters I brought into this world, who have seen me broken and still called me beautiful. You will find pieces of me in these pages that I once swore I'd never share. But healing asked for truth and my soul, tired of hiding, said yes.

There is a rhythm to my story, pauses where the heart catches its breath, storms where the soul barely stays afloat and quiet dawns that promise something better. I didn't always believe in the promise. Life had taught me to expect endings more than beginnings and even the brightest moments seemed borrowed, fleeting.

But somewhere beyond the pages I can see right now love will surprise me int the most lasting way. Not the love I chased before, but one that will stand still long enough for me to arrive. It will become my anchor, my soft place to land and in time, the truest chapter of all.

So, before the story begins, know this:

These words come from inner truth, not outside validation. This is a spiritual document. I did not write this to be seen; I wrote this as a torchlight for my daughters to follow so you could see yourselves and know that you are ever alone. That even in the mess there is meaning, and even in the dark, there is always a way back home.

Part One

Dear little me,

I see you.

I see the way you tried to be good, to be quiet, to be small hoping someone would finally notice how hard you were trying. I see the tears you swallowed, the questions you buried deep inside because no one seemed to have the answers you needed. I see the way you carried the weight of feeling unwanted, unworthy, unseen- long before you even knew what those words meant.

You were never too much

You were never not enough

You were never anything but pure and beautiful and deserving of every good thing.

I'm sorry the world didn't show you that. I'm sorry that love felt like something you had to chase or earn. I'm sorry, for every time you thought it was your fault. But I promise you this:

I'm here now

I am the woman you fought hard to become. I am the voice you never thought you'd find. I am the safe space you always needed. You don't have to be silent anymore. You don't have to be afraid. You don't have to keep carrying all that hurt alone.

We are healing

We are rising

We are learning that we were never broken, only bruised.

And most of all, you are loved.

You have always been loved.

Forever,

Me

Chapter 1

The Silence Before the Storm

"Not all storms come with thunder. Some arrive in silence and stay for years"

-Tamara Scott

This is the story of origin. Even in that quiet, the kind that doesn't leave bruises but still leaves scars something in me stirred. I knew there had to be more than this. That whisper became the fire I would later chase. But first, before the awakening came the quiet, and that's where my story truly begins.

There are silences that soothe, soft and sacred like a lullaby; and then there are silences that leave you wondering if anyone every truly saw you. Mine was the kind that smiled on the outside but never reached the heart. I didn't grow up around screaming or slammed doors. There was no war zone in my household, but there was also no warmth. I was told what to do but rarely, if ever, was told who I was or who I could become. I grew up in a home where love was spoken in silence. Not absent, but quiet in ways that mattered the most. Affection didn't flow freely but there were meals on the table, clothes on our backs, and rides to school; these were the offerings. I learned early how to translate the unspoken and I still remember the ache of never hearing the words I wanted to hear the most. Still, there were no warm hugs for no reason, those were rare, almost foreign and no "I love you" out of nowhere. Emotions were something you tucked away, not something you sat with. Love was more of a duty than a devotion and it never came the way I needed it; open, safe, and unconditional. "I love you" wasn't something you said it was something you were supposed to just know. As a child I didn't know how to name what was missing though. I just knew I felt a hunger I couldn't explain, a longing for warmth, comfort, safety, and softness. A deep ache in that, a kind of loneliness that made me question my worth before I even knew what self-worth meant. I needed the kind of love that not just keeps you alive but the kind that tells your soul it's safe to be seen here, the kind that wraps around you and said; You matter. You're seen. I'm proud of you. But the absence of love spoken out loud left its own scars. My needs didn't feel urgent enough. I was a little black girl with big glasses and gap teeth, receiving government assistance and struggling to find my place. My skin, my voice, my smile, all of it felt like too much and not enough at the same time. The world taught me very early that beauty, confidence, and value looked nothing like me. I didn't feel seen, not at home, not in classrooms, not even in mirrors. My voice didn't feel loud enough; and so, I learned to adapt, to perform, to be who I thought I needed to be to be accepted even if that meant silencing parts of myself to survive.

So, I shrank.

I was painfully shy, too timid to speak. Silence had already become my shield, it was the first language I learned, and not the soft kind. The kind that echoes when you cry in a room full of people and no one hears you. The kind that teaches you how to disappear without ever leaving. I was afraid to be noticed, afraid to take up any space that could draw judgement. Over time the silence stopped being a choice and it became who I was. But silence can be its own kind of violence. I didn't know how to express my voice, so I didn't. Not when I was hurt, not when I was proud, not when I needed something. I had learned to keep my needs hidden, my words buried, my truth locked tight inside. I learned early not to expect too much from anyone, to survive on scraps of connection. I learned how to sit still and not complain, how to carry disappointment in my chest without it showing in my eyes. I didn't ask for much, I learned how to be small, how to take up less space, how to keep quiet even when something in me was screaming for more. I didn't have a model for what love looked like, only what it wasn't. I didn't see tenderness between a man and a woman, I didn't see a strong, confident, black woman standing in her power, I didn't see vulnerability treated as strength. I saw survival, scraping by emotionally and making do with what little scraps of acknowledgement life offered. Because of that, I carried a deep ache into every part of my life and my understanding of what it means to feel seen.

I was the child who didn't cause trouble, who got good grades, who stayed in line. The "smart girl". That's what teachers called me, what other kids said, sometimes with admiration, sometimes with distance. I wore intelligence like a shield, learning early that answers could protect me when emotions couldn't. I took pride in my grades, in the certainty, in the structure. Homework turned in on time, straight A's, high honor roll certificates lined up like tiny affirmations that I mattered. But even perfection couldn't pull affection out of people who didn't know how to give it. My mind thrived but my soul ached quietly. It wasn't dramatic enough to be called trauma, but it was deep enough to shape every relationship that came after because when love isn't modeled out loud you grow up searching for echoes. You chase after people who are familiar, not necessarily safe. You try to earn love that should've been freely given and sometimes, you mistake silence for peace because it's what you've always known.

But there was one person I looked up to, my big sister. She was fire, voice, and presence. She said what was on her mind without fear, without apology. She wore her confidence like a crown. Even when she hurt, she made noise. She didn't disappear, and to a little girl who had forgotten how to speak, that looked like magic. She taught me things no one else did, she gave me glimpses of power even if I didn't yet know how to claim it for myself. And then there was my father, or more truthfully, the absence of him even when he was there. I was never taught what love from a man should look like. Not in how he spoke to me, not in how he showed up, not in how he treated the women around him. He didn't come to my school events, at least not one that I remember. I was a straight A student. Smart. Focused. I got invited to honor banquets, received certificates and medals with gold seals. Everyone else had their father present for their moment but that seat reserved for mines stayed empty. I wondered what else I had to do to be worth showing up for. I kept telling myself maybe next time, maybe if I get perfect grades again, maybe if I tried harder, I did better. But he still didn't come. So, the conclusion I came to wasn't about him, but about me. I must not be good enough; I must not matter. That ache never really left. It tucked itself into the corners of my confidence, it whispered into my relationships, it showed up every time I questioned my value. And as much as I wanted to believe I was worthy, the little girl in me kept asking the same quiet question.

Why wasn't I important enough for him to show up?

That question would follow me, leaving gaps in the places where tenderness should have lived. Especially when I began to search for love in men who weren't equipped to give it.

And then…there were moments that confused me even more, I was young, too young, when someone first touched me in a way that I didn't understand. It wasn't violent, it wasn't loud. That made it even harder to name. There was no scream, no broken door, no threat, just a shift in the air. A knowing in my body that said, this shouldn't be happening, but no one had ever told me how to respond. I didn't know how to tell anyone, I didn't even know how to tell myself. Was I supposed to feel special? Chosen? Loved? Because part of me wanted to be noticed, wanted to be seen, but not like that. Not in a way that made me want to hide my skin, hold my breath, and disappear.

And that's where the wires crossed.

Touch and love became tangled. Attention and discomfort blurred. Somewhere deep inside I began to wonder if this was what being "liked" meant. If discomfort was the price of connection. If silence was the only way to survive being wanted. I never got a lesson in the difference between love and harm, affection and control, admiration, and objectification. So I carried confusion with me, letting it shape how I received love, how I gave it and how I doubted whether I deserved it at all. No one sat me down to say love doesn't hurt, love doesn't shame you into silence, but that love holds you with care. I didn't see what a healthy relationship looked like or even how to be a friend because even friendships weren't modeled to me. I didn't know how to let others in or how to believe they would stay so I held people at a distance and made up the rules as I went; built on guesswork, survival, and longing. I watched the world and took notes, and I learned that sometimes love comes with pain. That silence could mean rejection, that affection could be earned or taken away. I didn't have a model for what it meant to be a strong Black woman either. Not the kind of strength that makes space for softness. The strength I saw was worn like armor, unbending, unyielding, necessary. I admired it but I feared it too. I wondered if being strong meant being alone, if it meant swallowing tears and pretending everything was fine. And when my voice started to crack from holding it all in, I got better at it.

Silence was survival.

The library became my refuge. Books didn't abandon. They didn't judge or misunderstand. Between those shelves I could become anyone, go anywhere, feel everything. Stories wrapped around me like warm blankets on cold days. I could sit for hours beneath the soft hum of fluorescent lights, hidden in corners consumed by other people's words because mine had nowhere to go. The characters felt more familiar than the people around me. Their struggles and triumphs whispered truths I hadn't yet found in my own life.

Reading gave me freedom, a space where I wasn't defined by the absence of what I needed but by the richness of what I could imagine. In those pages I found mirrors and windows, I saw versions of myself I didn't know existed and I started to believe I could become someone more than the roles I had been handed. Still even in that sacred silence a war raged inside me. I loved being alone, the independence, the peace of it, but I hated being by myself. Alone felt like a choice, by myself felt like punishment. Solitude became both sanctuary and a sentence. I learned to exist with the ache to swallow my longing for connection while pretending I didn't feel it at all.

These early lessons shaped everything and of course, no one tells you that when you grow up learning to be quiet, you also grow up believing your feelings are too loud to be loved and it affected how I saw people, how I let them treat me, and more importantly, how I treated myself. When I became a mother, I carried all of it with me, even when I tried not to. While my parents did what they could with what they had, what they didn't have was just as loud.

This is not a story of blame.

No one knew I was breaking because I was so good at building. Building masks, building walls, building futures in my mind that looked nothing like my reality. But inside, fractures were forming. Quietly. Deeply. Slowly.

This story reflects that ache and the long winding path I've walked to transform it into something softer, something sacred. A path I share now, not to rewrite the past but to offer you the truth of where I come from, about reclaiming the kind of love I never had and fought to learn to give to myself first, and then to you. So, if you're reading this now, my daughters or anyone who's ever questioned their worth because of what they didn't receive; I want you to know:

You were always worthy.

And I've learned to believe the same thing about myself.

Chapter 2

The Breaking Begins

I used to think breaking meant loud shatters and visible pieces. But mines was quiet. Like a teacup cracking beneath the paint, holding its shape until it didn't.

The silence that had shaped my childhood began to echo louder and in that echo the girl I was started slipping away, not all at once, but piece by piece, word by word, until the pages of my own story began to feel foreign to me. The breaking had begun.

I don't remember exactly when it happened.

Theres a stretch of time somewhere between eight and ten that exists like a blurred photograph in my mind. I can't see it clearly and I'm not sure I want to. I think I blocked it out.

When you experience sexual abuse as a child the lines between love, attention, and control get tangled. It taught two dangerous lies early on:

1. That my body held value
2. That attention, even the wrong kind, meant I mattered.

No one asked the right questions. I didn't have the words to tell anyone, I didn't know I could because even at that age I had already learned how to hold things in and all I had was shame and silence. Carrying a secret that felt too heavy for a child to carry.

Statistically I wasn't alone, according to the CDC, about 1 in 4 girls and 1 in 13 boys in the United States experience sexual abuse during childhood. Most of the time the abuser is someone you know and trust. But numbers can't capture the way it robs you of your innocence, how it takes away your ability to trust yourself, how it turns the most natural need, the need to be loved, into a lifelong battlefield. Or how it teaches you that your worth is tied to what someone can take from you and how shame disguises itself as desire. I didn't know what to call it back then. Sadness, anxiety, disconnection, I just knew something always felt heavy, like there was a weight in my chest I couldn't explain.

That's the thing about trauma; it doesn't always scream. Sometimes it whispers and waits curled up in the corners of memory, showing up when you're alone.

Even after my body had been touched in a way it never should have, I still had to get up and go to school. I still had to smile in pictures, do my homework, and sit in rooms with people who had no idea that a part of me had gone missing. And I didn't know how to get it back. While other kids played outside, rode bikes, or jumped rope in the summer heat, I stayed in my room. I wasn't grounded, just withdrawn. I no longer trusted touch, I stopped believing I was safe even in my own skin. It showed up in my need to always be in control, to always to achieve, to prove that I was still whole when I felt anything but.

I found comfort in silence, pages of notebooks filled with poems I never showed, drawings that held feelings I couldn't name. That was how I coped. Drawing let me say the things my mouth didn't know how to form. I didn't know I was coping I just thought that was who I was. But now I know I was managing emotions that no child should have to carry alone. There's a particular kind of pain in feeling invisible after being violated. A pain that grows louder when no one notices the change in your eyes or the sudden stillness in your voice. I was a child and I was broken in a way I couldn't explain. The world kept spinning and I learned to spin with it. Silently. Shamefully.

That was the first time my body stopped feeling like mine. The first time I questioned whether I was worth protecting and the beginning of a long, quiet war with myself, a war between the girl who wanted to be loved and the girl who didn't believe she deserved it anymore.

The library was still my sanctuary. I could disappear between the pages and not come out until I felt a little lighter. Even later in life, after heartbreak, after becoming a mother, after trauma; the library still felt like home. A place where I could breathe. I turned deeper into books. I sought out characters who had been hurt too, girls who had survived. I clung to their courage because I hadn't yet found my own.

As I grew up, I translated what had happened to me in survival tactics. Men like sex. If I gave them sex, they'll choose me and maybe they'll stay. I learned to weaponize my body, that being wanted physically was the only way I felt valuable. So, I played the part. I performed, I flirted, I stayed too long, I gave too much; and not because I wanted to, but because I thought I HAD to. I didn't want sex, I wanted comfort, I wanted to be chosen, I wanted safety, I wanted the ache to stop. And that confusion led me to choices that echoed pain I was never allowed to speak aloud. I became hypersexual because something sacred in me had been stolen. I was trying to get it back the only way I knew how and I would spend years trying to control what was once taken from me. I couldn't tell the difference between being wanted and being used or between love and lust. By the age of 13 I was pregnant. I wasn't reckless, I wasn't stupid, I wasn't too "loose", or fast but because I was wounded. Somewhere inside me I believed that being wanted, even in the most broken way, was better than being invisible. No one asked if I was ready, it was just unspoken that I would keep the baby. No one asked if I was healed, if I felt supported, if I even knew who I was. One minute I was a girl trying to make sense of my own broken childhood and the next I was holding life in my belly, life that didn't ask to be born but would need everything I didn't have yet. Motherhood came like a wave that I couldn't stop and instead of drowning, I learned how to float through chaos. No one ever asks, "what happened?" "What went wrong?" they just look and judge. The truth is yes, what happened to me confused my relationship with sex, yes it made me chase pleasure to distract from pain, yes, I used my body when I didn't know how to use my voice. That switch was already switched; the lines were so blurred there was no line. Pleasure versus pain, choice versus conditioning, it felt like a transaction more than a connection. I said yes when I wanted to say no, I smiled when I wanted to cry. I let people touch my body because I didn't know how to protect my heart. People saw me and made assumptions. They saw the confidence, the curves, the boldness, but they didn't see the real truth. The girl inside, still scared, still ashamed, still pretending to be someone she wasn't, still wondering why her earliest memories of affection came with confusion and guilt. I gave so many pieces of me away and I kept hoping the right person would see me, hold me differently, and return some of those missing pieces back to me but I didn't realize I was holding myself with judgement.

But I see her now.

The young girl who thought she had to earn love with skin, who carried silence like a second name. She doesn't need to be ashamed anymore. It took time. Therapy. Tears. Unlearning. It took naming the trauma out loud. And now I know she just needed someone to tell her the truth:

You are not what happened to you, that was not your fault, and it should've never happened. You are not wrong for craving connection. You are not dirty, broken, or beyond healing. That wasn't love. My body is mine. My no means no. My yes is sacred, and I never have to perform to be loved. I am more than my wounds. I am more than who touched me, hurt me, abandoned me. You are a woman learning how to come home to herself and now, you get to choose what love looks and feels like. I am a woman reclaiming her power, and now, every inch of me belongs to me.

No one told me. So, standing in the doorway of my own life, watching it in a blur, I realized the version of me that still believed love could fix things, that trust was enough, and that someone would notice the pain if it got loud enough, she started fading. The breaking never really stopped, it just slowed down, almost imperceptible ways I disappeared into what people needed me to be. I remember coming across the line "She didn't speak of it, but it lived in her like a second heartbeat." I held onto that line like it was a scripture. It told me I wasn't the only one. I still don't remember everything, but I remember enough to know it changed me. I write it down now not to relive it, but to release it because silence protected me once; but it also kept me locked inside my own pain.

And I'm done being loyal to my suffering.

They called it resilience; I called it survival.

Breathe.

Turn the page when you are ready.

Chapter 3

Becoming What I Wasn't

There are some roles we step into before our souls are ready. Not because we choose them, but because life hands us a script and no time to rehearse.

There's a sound I still can't forget.

Not the sound of my own heartbeat when I saw the pregnancy test, not the whispers in the hallway at school, but the sound of my mama's cry when she found out.

I had just came out of the bathroom but it was like time froze. I didn't even have the words before the truth beat me to it. She ran from the bathroom to the front room and collapsed on the floor like the wind had been knocked out of her spirit. I stood there frozen, watching the woman who carried me, raised me, break right in front of me.

I didn't know what to do.

I heard her say to my aunt "What am I going to do?" and those words hit me harder than any punishment ever could. I wanted to disappear. I wanted to take it all back. I felt horrible. I felt ashamed, like I failed her, like I failed me. Even though I was the one carrying the baby it felt like we were both carrying the shame.

No one talks about that kind of silence. The kind where love doesn't disappear but disappointment fills the room like smoke. Its hard to breathe in it. I couldn't even cry. My tears were stuck behind guilt; all the wishing, all the wondering what could've been different.

Three children followed, all before marriage, all by separate men, and each one a complicated mixture of pain, hope, and survival. I became a mother before I even had the chance to figure out how to be a child or a teenager. What little identity I had, it disappeared the moment I gave birth to my first child. I loved my babies fiercely, how I looked at myself, I never looked at them. They became the reason I kept going when everything inside me wanted to give up. I made a silent vow long before they were born, that none of them, my daughters especially, would never have to guess their worth.

I didn't know how to parent when I first became a mother. Mothering, nurturing, that came naturally to me, but *parenting*, knowing how to guide, protect, empower, I was lost. I knew I wanted to give them everything I didn't have, not just love but freedom, not just protection, but power. I didn't know then that it also came with silent sacrifices, the kind that no one claps for. The early days of my twenties were rough. I was still a child inside, raising children of my own and now another added pressure, being a wife. There were too many days where I sat in the dark, while everyone slept, silently grieving the girl I never got to be. My daughters were born from the parts of me that refused to stay silent, the parts that still believed in magic, healing, and rising again. I didn't want them to have to survive the way I did; I wanted them to thrive. Postpartum depression wrapped itself around me like a heavy fog and no one ever talked about it, at least not in the surroundings I knew. I thought I was just weak, only tired, just bad at being a mother. I see it differently now. I was overwhelmed, I was drowning, and no one had thrown a life raft. I faked it every day, year after year. They didn't see the shame, the loneliness, the pressure to prove I wasn't just another statistic. They didn't hear the voice in my head whispering: *You're already failing*. I knew to be able to teach them truly, it wasn't just about me telling them, I knew I had to unlearn my own fears, break my own chains, so that when I looked at them, they would see a woman who was free and know that they could too. Teaching them to fly had meant unlearning the things I once believed: that love must be earned, that silence is safer, that black girls must shrink themselves to survive.

No.

My daughter will know their voices mattered, that their dreams aren't too big, that their magic isn't something to apologize for. That they are limitless, That "no" is a full sentence. Period. That being soft is not a weakness, being black is not a burden, it is a crown. And every time I teach them to trust their own wings, I heal a piece of the girl I once was, the girl who needed someone to teach her how to soar.

Here's the part that I only understood years later. My mother wasn't crying because she hated me. She was crying because she *loved* me. Because she knew how hard the road would be, because she wanted more for me, not less. And because in that moment she saw the little girl she raised about to walk a woman's road she hadn't been prepared for. Back then I didn't have the words for that. Back then I just felt small. Unworthy. Like my life was over before it started but that moment shaped me, not just as a mother but as a daughter. It taught me what it feels like to break someone's heart without meaning to. It also taught me that healing something starts at the very place where everything cracked.

Letter to my younger self:

Hey baby girl,

I see you.

Standing there with swollen eyes and a heavy heart trying to be everything for everyone before you've even figured out who you are. You're scared, I know. Scared of failing, scared of becoming the woman you swore you wouldn't. Scared of repeating pain that was passed down like an unwanted gift. You feel alone even when people are around and you're carrying more than any young girl should have to carry. Fear, disappointment, shame and this unspoken pressure to never mess up, even when no one is guiding you. But I need you to know something,

You are not broken.

You are becoming.

You are not your mother's mistakes.

You are not your father's absence.

You are not the sum of your heartbreaks or the silence you were forced to swallow.

You are powerful.

You are worthy.

You are more than enough, even on the days you feel invisible. You think no one sees you, but I do. I see the fight in your eyes, the way you love even when it hurts, the way you keep showing up when all you want to do is hide. I wish I could reach through life and hold your hand. Tell you to rest. Breathe. To stop trying so hard to earn love that should've been yours for free. One day, you'll become the woman you always needed.

Not perfect, but whole

I love you; I forgive you, I'm so proud of you! Keep going she's waiting for you on the other side.

-*ME*

My beautiful girls,

There are some things this world will try to teach you and some things I want you to remember, especially if you ever find yourself walking into motherhood before you're ready. I became a mother too soon.

I was young, still trying to find my voice while raising tiny humans who needed answers I didn't have yet. I did the best I could with what I knew, but the truth is, I was growing up while I raised you. And that kind of love is messy, deep, imperfect, and real. If you ever find yourself in that place, pregnant, unsure, and trying to figure out who you are while caring for someone else, listen closely:

You are not a failure.

You are not ruined.

You are not alone.

Motherhood doesn't cancel your dreams. It just gives you new reasons to chase them. It's ok to be tired, to cry, to not have it all figured out. It's ok to ask for help, to take a break, to choose yourself sometimes. That does not make you selfish, it makes you human. And when you start doubting whether you are doing enough, remember, love is not measured in perfection. It is felt in your presence, your honesty, and your willingness to grow alongside your child.

Please don't forget to care for you.

You were someone before you became "mom" and that girl still matters. She still needs to be nurtured, protected, and reminded that her life is valuable too. You can break generational cycles and still rest, you can be a good mother and still need space. You can choose peace, even if the world around you doesn't understand your choices. I hope you always remember that being a mother is not your only identity, but it is a sacred one. Its one that will stretch you, shake you, and show you how strong you truly are.

And not matter what, whether you decide to become a mother, a woman on the edge of discovery, or just trying to find your way, I am always with you. Cheering. Covering. Loving.

With all my love,

Mom

Part Two

Chapter 4

Love in Disguise

"Commitment without connection is just quiet suffering dressed up as loyalty."

-Author unknown

The search for love took me into the arms of men, but not into the arms of myself. My early romantic experiences were fraught with insecurities and a desperate need for validation. Red flags were there but I ignored them. By the time I was twenty years old I thought marriage would finally fix the ache inside me. I wasn't marrying for survival, for validation, for help. I was already a mother of three. Three beautiful reasons to fight for a better life. Three innocent faces looking to me for answers I didn't yet have. Society whispered that marriage was the right next step, the proof that I was still "good enough" to be a wife, even after becoming a mother before saying "I do". I wanted the safety; I wanted the title. I wanted to believe that maybe I hadn't ruined my chances at being loved. I needed to believe that. I unconsciously sought out men who reinforced my feelings of inadequacy and mirrored my trauma. So when the chance came,

I married him.

A man who made promises he couldn't keep, promises I desperately clung to. A man who cheated and lied and I tried to forgive because I was terrified of being alone again. Terrified that if this didn't work, it meant it was permanently broken. And when the betrayals started to stack up, part of me raged at him but another part quietly wondered:

Was it really all his fault if I didn't even know what love was supposed to look like? How can I give someone something I never had? Something I couldn't even give myself? How can I chase something I don't understand?

The truth was I hadn't married him because I loved him deeply, I married him because I was scared and desperate to be saved. I was desperate for help and scared that no one else would want me. Desperate for a chance at the life I thought I had already disqualified from. I thought this was my only chance to be seen as whole. When that marriage fell apart, it cracked me open, it broke the little hope I had left. And instead of taking the time to heal me, I stumbled, sprinted rather, into another storm, a second marriage.

The worst decision of my life.

It wasn't just unhealthy; it was abusive in every way that mattered. It wasn't the loud fights that told the truth. It was the silences. A relationship built on control, fear, manipulation, and pain. He broke things in me I didn't even know were still intact. There were days when I didn't recognize my own face in the mirror, my own voice in the arguments, even my own dreams shriveled into silence. The love I had spent so long chasing had turned into a cage. The way he could say "I love you" with his mouth but his eyes never joined in the chorus. There was no love, just a perverse imitation of it. I learned early that love could sound right and feel wrong. There were so many bad choices, so many reckless moments born from brokenness, so many scars layered over each other that I stopped being able to tell where the newest one began. I accepted it because it matched the ache I had carried since childhood, like, this is all I deserve, this is all I am worth. I didn't love myself enough to leave in that moment, but I knew I didn't want my babies to continue to see it. I didn't want them to stick around and let it ever become a point where his anger starts to shift and be directed to any of them. I sent them to live with my mother. And I continued to stay longer than I should have, I stayed because the world taught me that leaving meant failure. That good women endured. I stayed because "I love you" was the only apology he knew how to give, and I was still the girl who wanted to believe that was enough.

But the body doesn't lie. My shoulders were always tight, my chest always braced, my spirit always calculating when it was safe to speak and when it was safer to disappear inside myself. I survived longer than I thought I could and eventually I escaped. It wasn't even because I believed I deserved better, it was that I realized the full extent of what he was capable of, what he could do but had not yet.

He could kill me.

I can still hear the gunshot, the whiz of it passing by my ear, the ringing in my ears that stayed for what seemed like forever. He felt no remorse, oh no, he wasn't sorry at all. I had to go, and I had to go *now*! That night I left with nothing but what I could fit in my car and my will to survive. I found myself staying in cheap motels, clutching to what little sense of safety I created for myself. It was there, in that lonely in between space, that I met the man who would become my third husband.

He wanted to rescue me. He saw a broken woman, bruised, tired, lost and offered a hand to pull me out of the wreckage. We became friends; he showed me what peace looked like. I admired his strength, his drive, his resilience, and his determination to succeed. I thought I was in love and I wanted him to love me the same way. I was so desperate for it that I was willing to work for even scraps of it, I worked for it like a job. I would clean his house, scrub baseboards, wash dishes, do whatever I could to stay close, to be near him, to be wanted, to matter, to be needed.

I confused service with worthiness.

I confused my presence with affection.

I confused proximity with love.

Every time he let me in it felt like a small victory but every time he pulled away it reignited the old, familiar ache of not being enough. Truth is, I wasn't looking for a partner back then; I was still looking for a savior. Still believing that if I could just be good enough, helpful enough, loyal enough, pretty enough, sexy enough.... Someone would finally choose me without conditions. My self-worth was so low, so fragile, that I accepted this behavior as a form of love. I didn't know what a healthy relationship looked like, that was foreign to me. I was still too busy trying to prove my worth to him, to the world, and most of all to myself. Even in those early days the seeds of a harder truth were already planted:

No one can save you from wounds you haven't faced yourself. I just wanted to feel like the first thought, not the background voice. I wanted to be adored and not just included. That wasn't just heartbreak, that was undiagnosed anxiety wrapped in abandonment wounds.

Looking back, I see the disguise now. Love does not make you small. Love does not take from you without giving something back. Love is not a game of survival. I had mistaken the intensity of the fire for its warmth, and I almost burned away the woman I was meant to become.

And the love I thought it had, I finally found, was about to reveal even more lessons I hadn't yet learned. I didn't know it yet but somewhere down the road love will find me in a way I've never known before. Not the kind that burns hot and burns out, not the kind that asks to lose myself to keep it alive- but the kind that teaches me, gently, that I am safe. It will grow slowly, without disguise or pretense until one day I realize that I am home.

That love will become my final chapter in this part of the story, my safe harbor after years of restless waters. It will be patient with my scars, kind to my healing, and strong enough to weather every storm beside me. I won't see it coming but it will turn out to be my best and last love, the place where my heart can finally rest.

You deserve to be adored. Not just tolerated, not just needed, but seen, cherished, held in awe for your light, your softness, your strength, and your truth.

The desire to be adored is not vanity, it's the soul's reminder of what it came here to receive. You want to be adored because you were made for that level of love. The kind that doesn't just touch your body but bows to your energy; the kind that holds you sacred.

Here's the truth:

You don't have to beg for what your spirit was built to attract. You just have to stay in alignment with the version of you who knows her worth and won't shrink it for anyone who doesn't.

Let that be your standard now. Let adoration be your birthright, because it is.

Chapter 5

The Mirror Shatter

"I fell by your force…. but I'll rise from my own ashes"

-Author unknown

Sometimes there are moments in life when something inside you breaks so sharply, so unmistakably that you know, without question, you'll never be or even look at yourself the same again. This was that moment for me. I asked my daughter a single question. One I wish I could erase, left my lips. A man I trusted, I thought I loved, twisted my mind into believing things no mother should believe. I didn't fight hard enough. I didn't walk away fast enough. I never should have asked it and it wasn't because I didn't love her, but because the storm inside me was still echoing with the silence of my own childhood. The moment she said no, it was like a thread snapped inside me, and somewhere deep down I knew.

This was not love. This was not ok.

Nothing happened to her but something happened to me. Something shifted. The guilt settled in and became part of my skin. It was mine. The moment was mine. The breaking…that was all mine. But now, now I know that guilt was never mine to carry alone. I was a mother with unmothered wounds. A girl in a woman's body still trying to survive the storm. The words weren't truly mine. They were shaped by fear, by trauma, by a man who chipped away at me and made me question my own voice until it echoed his. I knew it was wrong the moment it left my mouth. I saw the confusion in her eyes, the shift in her spirit. I felt something inside me fracture.

That question was never who I am, but it did become the mirror that showed me who I had let myself become. I carried that moment with me. I carried it through sleepless nights full of guilt and through the silence I kept afterwards, not knowing how to make it right. The silence after I said it was heavier than anything I had ever carried. It was under the influence of this man that I learned how easy it is to become someone you don't recognize. I'd wandered so far from myself. Abuse doesn't always show up as bruises, although I had those too. Sometimes it shows up as manipulation so deep it rewrites your instincts. I stopped trusting myself and at that moment I betrayed myself, and her. But that also was the moment I woke up. The mirror didn't just crack that day, it fell to the ground and shattered. The mirror didn't lie; it shattered because it could no longer hold all of my denial. The shattering wasn't the end. It was the start of the becoming. I packed up my pain, my guilt, my exhaustion and I took my kids to my mother's. It felt like betrayal once again, to leave them there, but I didn't have anything else to give yet. I knew it was time to go. I couldn't stay with a man I had once believed would protect me, who instead dismantled me piece by piece.

I still remember the trembling in my body, shaking from fear. The sound of the bullet, knowing that it narrowly missed hitting me. And I just knew that next time he wouldn't miss.

I had no home and no plan, only the decision that staying would destroy what little I had left. I moved into a motel. Just me, my thoughts, and the kind of silence that screams. The silence felt like punishment, like a courtroom where I was both the accused and the judge. I remember the coldness of the room, the flickering light, the weight of the empty bed, and the sound of the traffic outside the windows that somehow echoed the chaos I was trying to leave behind. I sat on the edge of the bed, staring at nothing. The hardest part wasn't the loneliness; it was the separation from my kids. The motel walls held my grief like a secret. I cried most nights. Ashamed, confused, yet stubbornly clinging to the hope that I was doing the right thing, even if it didn't feel like it.

I wrestled with regret constantly. Not just for the question, not just for what I allowed, but for the time I could never get back. For the version of me that didn't know how to fight better for herself. For the girl inside me that no one had protected- and who didn't how to protect others either. I mouthed it silently, then whispered to the air "I'm sorry". No one was there to hear it but I wasn't saying it for anyone else. I was saying it for my daughter hoping that somehow she could feel the truth in my spirit even if I couldn't say it to her the way I wanted to. I was saying it for the woman I was becoming, for the mother who finally chose to face herself. The motel, as painful as it was, became sacred ground. It was where I started to remember, where I heard my own voice again in the silence. Where I cried out to God, to my ancestors, to my

Ori- asking for forgiveness, for guidance, for strength. Its where I began to journal again, it wasn't poetic or perfect, I needed to get the weight out of my head. I wrote letters I never sent, I wrote prayers, I wrote to my children, and I wrote to the version of myself that I had abandoned. Regret doesn't vanish with apologies, it lingers.

But then I started to feel something shift. A subtle unbinding like the chains of shame had loosened just enough to let breath in and slowly I began to feel pieces returning to me. The mirror had shattered, yes, but that season in the motel was when I learned how to pick up the shards without cutting myself open. It was the beginning of returning home to myself. There was no quick healing, no easy redemption, just the long slow unfolding of truth.

My daughter? She became one of the greatest teachers, even in silence. Even in pain she reminded me that love can be returned to and that healing though imperfect, is always possible. I write this to say:

I forgive myself.

I see myself.

I will never be silent again.

This chapter isn't just about guilt. It's about reckoning. It's about ownership. It's about the holy work of rising from a broken place, of standing barefoot in the ruins of the woman I once was and choosing to rebuild-this time from truth.

Excerpt:

No one talks about the heartbreak of motherhood. The kind where your own child becomes the source of your deepest wound.

I never imagined a day where my child would become the one to lay hands on me.

A split eyebrow.

A busted lip.

A black eye.

A concussion.

And a heart so shattered that, once again, I didn't recognize myself in the mirror. That fight broke something in me, not just physically but spiritually, I cried like a little girl in the shower that night- not because of the pain but because of the grief. Because deep down inside, it was my fault how we got here. Because I didn't know if we'd ever come back from it. Because part of me still saw the quiet little boy who used to curl up next to me when he was scared; and I couldn't find him anymore. Those days were heavy. I moved through them like a ghost tending to everything and everyone except myself. Until one day, I stopped. I sat with the truth: I was not ok. It took years, years, to forgive. But I did, not just for him, for me. Because I couldn't keep bleeding from a wound I refused to look at.

Chapter 6

Gathering All the Pieces

"There are some wounds we don't speak of because we're afraid the truth will make us unlovable. But healing begins the moment we stop hiding."

-Sharon Jaynes

There are wounds you expect to get in motherhood. Sleepless nights, heartbreak over their heartbreak, silent sacrifices they may never understand. But nothing prepares you for the kind of pain that comes when your own child turns on you.

I shattered all over again, what progress and strength I had started to build was gone again. It wasn't just the slap of skin or the sudden weight of his fist hitting my face, it was the sound of my heart breaking from the inside out. A concussion made the room spin for days, but that didn't compare to the ache in my chest. This wasn't a stranger. This wasn't a man I could walk away from. This was my son.

The boy I held in my arms as a baby. The one I nursed from my own breasts. The one I nurtured when he had a fever. The one I stayed up late worrying about. The one I tried to protect from this very kind of pain- and now, he was handing it back to me. No one tells you what to do when that happens. I remember sitting in the shower that night, blood and tears running down the drain. I cried because I felt like a failure. I cried because I blamed myself. I cried because I stayed too long with an abusive man that my own child is starting to mirror him. I cried because I part of me still wanted to protect him…even from himself. The fight didn't just leave permanent bruises on my body; it left bruises on my spirit. I questioned everything. I questioned my motherhood. I questioned my worth, I questioned whether I had broken him or if the world had. And the shame, God the shame. I didn't want to talk about it, didn't want to admit that my own child had done this. There is a silent rule in motherhood that says we don't speak on the ugly parts, but silence is a slow death, and I had wanted to disappear into silence again, like I had as a child.

This was not the way love was supposed to feel. This was not the mother I imagined I would be.

I saw myself in him. The same rage, the same helplessness, the same silence that I had carried from my own childhood into my womanhood. But I also saw something else, the generational echo of trauma, passed down like a curse no one wanted but everyone seemed to carry. That night wasn't just about my son hurting me. It was about the mirror being held up to everything I had avoided facing.

I signed my rights over to his father.

Not out of anger, but out of heartbreak and self-preservation. I couldn't protect him anymore and I couldn't keep sacrificing myself in the name of love that didn't feel safe anymore. He apologized days later. Through text. But we haven't spoken since. Not fully. And that left a scar so deep I wasn't sure it would ever close.

With time though, I forgave. It wasn't quick and it wasn't clean. And it wasn't a conversation. Some days I had to forgive him all over again. But I had to forgive because I couldn't keep bleeding from a wound I wasn't willing to face. I forgave him for not knowing what to do with his anger. I forgave myself for not stopping it sooner. I forgave the universe for giving me a son with a pain I couldn't fix. Forgiveness doesn't mean I excused it, it just meant I chose peace over bitterness. It meant I chose me. And that choice?

That was the beginning of my real healing.

It wasn't pretty. It wasn't quick. It was tears, therapy sessions, prayers whispered through clenched teeth, and journal pages soaked with sorrow. It was realizing that forgiveness had to flow both ways- from me to him, and from me to myself.

That fight broke me, yes, but it also cracked me open and in the breaking I began to gather the pieces; not just of myself, but of my family. Love, I learned is not only in the gentle moments. Sometimes its in the rebuilding after the destruction, in the courage to name what happened and choose a different story moving forward.

This is where my motherhood shifted from survival to intention. From carrying pain to breaking cycles. From silence to speaking, even when my voice shook.

The fight that broke me also gave me the chance to remake myself.

My son,

I keep asking myself, where did I fail you? Where did I lose you? And now I'm at a crossroad no mother wants to face; no mother ever wants to experience. Signing over my rights. My right to be your parent, your provider, your protecter, your nurturer. Not because I don't love you, but because I must save what's left of me. I'm choosing survival and it breaks my heart to do it. We haven't spoken, not really. Maybe we wont for a long time, but even as I sit in the stillness of this pain, I feel something else rising.

Anger

Because this is not ok. Because it destroyed something inside of me, but if I don't forgive you, and myself, I'll never breathe free again. Still, I'm mad! For the anger you gave me that you couldn't name, for the blow you can't take back, for the silence that followed. I'm mad at myself, for not knowing how to stop it, for staying quiet too long. For loving you so much that I forgot to protect my own heart. I don't know what comes next, I don't know if we will ever heal this. Bu even now, you are still my son. And I will always love you, even from a distance.

-Mom

Anger

Anger is not a weakness. It's a response to being unheard. To being disrespected. To being abandoned, betrayed, or dismissed. Sometimes anger is the voice we never had as a child. It's the scream we swallowed. The "how dare you" that never left our lips.

You have every right to feel it.

Especially if you were expected to forgive before you were ever allowed to grieve. Especially if people acted like you were the problem for finally speaking up. But holding onto anger for too long becomes a prison. A place where pain lives on repeat. And you-you deserve to be free.

Forgiveness

Forgiveness doesn't mean forgetting. It doesn't excuse the wound or deny the damage. It just says: This pain will not own me anymore. Its reclaiming your energy, its choosing peace. Not because they deserve it, but because you do. You don't have to speak to them, you don't have to trust them again. You just have to stop carrying what's too heavy to hold any longer.

Fragments on the Floor

Glass was not the only thing that shattered that night.

My body bruised, my spirit cracked, my son's voice still ringing in the air like a siren I could not silence.

I picked up the pieces, not of the broken things scattered across the room but of myself.

Each shard whispered a question:

Where did this rage begin?

Whose hands first taught us how to hurt?

How many mothers have been broken by the sons they raised?

How many sons are carrying the storms of fathers who never showed up?

I held the fragments in my hands and they cut me open again. But even in the bleeding, I saw a chance to piece together a new kind of love, one not built on silence and survival, but on the truth I had avoided for too long.

Sometimes it takes a break so deep to remember that love is worth rebuilding.

Part Three

Chapter 7

Daughters of My Soul

"In you I see my renewal- my legacy made whole."

-Author unknown

To my daughters, you are the love I longed for, the strength I grew for, and the future I fought for. You were my first true sunrise, the light that broke across my soul when I thought I would never see morning again. You taught me that love is not pain, not fear, not a transaction- but a river, endless and patient, washing everything clean. You taught me that healing is not about forgetting but remembering who I truly am. You are the parts of me that survived. You are the dreams I built with my bare hands. You are the miracle that pushed me to believe again. This chapter, this journey, this life, I give it to you. May you carry the fire and the tenderness, the strength and the softness, the truth and the love, everywhere you go. I love you beyond this lifetime, and every lifetime after.

Girls, listen to me. If y'all ever only read one chapter of this book, let it be this one. This is the chapter I prayed you'd read one day. If you skip the rest of this book, I can live that but don't skip this. This is my heart. Raw, open and full of love laid bare before you.

I've lived through storms I never wanted you to feel; but some you caught wind of anyway. I can't undo that. I can't rewrite the past but I can give you my truth so you don't have to learn the hard way like I did.

Becoming your mother reshaped me at my very core, it rebuilt me completely. When I became a mother, I thought I had to be perfect. I didn't always know what I was doing, there was no guidebook handed to me, no blueprint, I was only fourteen. You all taught me that love isn't about getting everything right but about showing up repeatedly, even when it's hard. Even when you're tired. Even when you're afraid. You taught me that healing is a daily choice and not a final destination and that sometimes the most sacred thing a woman can do is to break the cycle she was born into. A story I wanted to rewrite before y'all were born, a promise I desperately tried so hard to keep.

My daughters would not inherit my pain.

Not to inherit the silence I was forced to swallow, not the shame I was made to carry, not the loneliness I was taught to normalize. They would not inherit the version of love that came with bruises, and not the definition of strength that meant suffering alone. Instead, they would inherit the sound of their own voice being honored, the feeling of arms that hold you without hurting you, the memory of being celebrated, not erased. I chose to break what needed to be broken so that they could be whole. Every late night, every early morning, every tear I never showed you, every prayer I whispered- they were spells cast in your name. They were bricks laid for a foundation I never had, but you would.

There are no words wide enough, deep enough, or bright enough to fully capture what you have given me. Still, I am writing because you deserve to know. You taught me what no one else could do:

What real, true love feels like.

Not the love that demands, judges, or leaves, but the love that stays. The love that opens without fear. The love that believes, even when the world tries to make them doubt.

You have watched me struggle. You've seen me tired, torn, and sometimes too quiet to explain why. I know there were days where you wondered where Mama went but the truth is I was trying to find her too. I have made mistakes, plenty of them, I have broken in front of you, I've had to make decisions that hurt us all. Everything I did, even when it was messy, was rooted in love. The kind of love that said you deserve more than a mother running on empty. I have loved you the best way I knew how. Sometimes that was enough and sometimes it wasn't; But it was always real. I tried to give you everything I had and everything I had to teach myself along the way.

I didn't want you to spend decades unlearning what I never should have been taught. I planted seeds and I wanted them to be good seeds. Of truth. Of worthiness. Seeds of permission to be fully yourselves-loud, soft, angry, brilliant, whatever you needed to be.

Through the laughter, the tears, the stubbornness, and the beauty, you both gave me the clearest mirror to see my own heart. You taught me about healing. That healing doesn't come from pretending but from honesty. From saying "I don't know yet but I'm trying" from getting up after falling, from letting love patch the wounds life left behind, from forgiving myself. Watching you grow taught me that being a mother is messy, courageous, and holy. It gives you strength that no book can ever explain, the kind of strength that wakes up before the sun, that fights silent battles, that sacrifices without applause. I didn't know how much fire lived inside me until I had to keep y'all warm. I didn't know how much hope I could hope until I saw it flicker in your eyes, I didn't know how soft, how fierce, how relentless love could be- until you.

For a while I lost it. The fire, the strength, the hope. But I knew y'all deserved better and through healing I rebuilt myself. Again. I had to tear down the walls I built around my heart, burn away the false identities the world gave me, crack open the places I thought were dead.

I found strength in my softness. I found pride in my vulnerability, I found power in simply being who I was fully, and without apology. Through you I understood:

Motherhood is not the erasing of the woman- it is the awakening of the Empress inside her and because of you:

I stand taller

I feel deeper

I believe in magic again,

Y'all are, and always will be, my greatest teachers. And sometimes, the greatest love I could offer you wasn't teaching you to be perfect, it was teaching you that being real was enough.

They are proof that we can be both the wound and the healing, the dream and the dreamer, the flame and the light. My gorgeous daughters, I hope I gave you space to speak your truth, permission to feel your feelings, roots deep enough to weather the storm and wings wide enough to fly beyond my dreams for you. Where I was silenced, you roar.

Where I was overlooked, you shine.

Where I was broken, you build.

I need you to remember:

You are not here to be small.

You are not here to shrink yourself so other people feel big.

You are not here to prove that you are worthy.

You were born worthy and life will try to convince you otherwise. People will lie to you, betray you, love you only when it benefits them and walk away when it doesn't. Don't let that make you doubt yourself. I need you to remember:

1. Your body is not an apology. You don't owe it to anyone.
2. Your heart is a treasure. Guard it like its gold.
3. Your mind is yours. Keep learning, keep questioning, keep thinking for yourself.
4. Your spirit is sacred. Don't let anyone dim it to make themselves more comfortable.

You will mess up, you will trust the wrong people, you will love someone who hurt you; that's life. But what you do next, how you get back up, how you heal, how you choose again; That's what will define you.

Don't be afraid to walk away from anything that breaks your peace and don't stay anywhere just because you're scared to start over. I promise starting over is survivable. If you ever doubt how strong you are, remember this:

You come from a woman who had nothing left but kept going. You come from a line of women who've been underestimated, overlooked, and counted out, and still stood back up. If you forget everything else, I've said hold onto this:

You are not repeating my story but re-writing your own and that, my loves, is the most sacred victory of all. Every time you laugh without fear, every time you say "No" to what doesn't serve you, every time you choose yourself first- you are healing not just yourself, but the generations that came before you. Because of you my bloodline is not a curse. It is a garden. And you, my daughters, are the wildflowers that grew even in places no one thought could bloom. If there is another life after this one, if there is another sky we cross, another Earth we walk- I would still choose you. I would find you and I would love you both all over again. Because you didn't just make me a mother.

You made me whole.

You made me alive.

You made me free.

And for that, I will spend the rest of my life and whatever comes after loving you with gratitude too big for words. You are enough. You are loved. And there is nothing you can do to make me stop loving you. You are my daughters. You are my soul. And my soul? She's unstoppable.

Chapter 8

Love, Redefined

"I carry within me all the generations I come from. Their struggles, their triumphs, their magic"

Sometimes what breaks you isn't the end,
it's the beginning of your return.

They say a woman doesn't rise until she's fallen completely apart. If that's true, then I must've been buried under the rubble of my own life. There were days when I couldn't find a reason to get out of bed and nights when I hoped I wouldn't wake up. I attempted to leave this world multiple times because I couldn't carry the weight of it all. The pain, the shame, the exhaustion. I failed in those attempts and for a long time that felt like another failure too. My smile became a mask stretched tightly over silent screams. I wore strength like armor in public. I worked when I wanted to run. Said "I'm fine" when I was falling apart. I kept showing up, mothering, working, surviving, but inside I was splintering. Quietly. Constantly. My mental breakdowns didn't come all at once, I splintered quietly over the years of pretending. Some subtle and slow, others loud and devastating. I would be folding laundry or brushing my teeth and suddenly I'd feel the panic crawling up my spine like a fire I couldn't put out. I'd lock myself in the bathroom just to cry in silence. No one could know. I had to be strong.

But I wasn't.

When life finally cracked all the way open, I couldn't pretend anymore. Pretend I wasn't tired, pretend I wasn't scared. Pretend that I had it all under control. Everything was unraveling in silence. Motherhood made me strong, but it also buried me beneath expectations no one saw. Everything collapsed. My kids saw me upright but inside I was falling. The weight of my past, the trauma no one ever apologized for, the heartbreaks I never healed from. I couldn't give them the version of me they deserved while I was drowning. That broke me in ways I still can't fully understand. It felt like this was starting to be a habit. It felt like I couldn't even take care of my own kids. It felt like I just couldn't get it right. It felt like I didn't even deserve the title of "Mother." I walked away from them, not out of abandonment but out of desperation to find the pieces of myself I had lost in everyone else's needs. All of it began to echo louder than my will to keep going. That's when I knew it wasn't just sadness; this was something deeper. The exhaustion wasn't just physical, it was mental. Emotional. Spiritual. I was grieving the woman I had to become just to survive.

Admitting I needed help wasn't easy. Not as a Black woman, not as a mother, not as someone always seen as strong. But I did.

I walked myself into the facility to check for mental illness, I bared my soul, all of it, and by speaking my truth finally out loud, I went to the psych ward. It wasn't voluntary and I wasn't happy, but I surrendered. I wasn't weak nor crazy, I was done carrying things alone.

When I walked through the doors of the psychiatric unit I was broken and scared and numb. The room was cold and sterile, but it was quiet. For the first time in a long time I was in a place where I couldn't run, perform, or hide. That terrified me. I cried the first night, I hated the beige walls and how small I felt in a paper gown but by the morning, something shifted. The universe had already begun to orchestrate my restoration. A patient discharging that day gave me a book and I didn't know then but that book would help reawaken my spiritual self. It gave language to the battles I'd fought silently for years. The book? Its called "The Chronicles of Ori" by Harmonia Rosales. Something in me stirred, Ori, I had just learned not too long prior to my stay, is the spiritual consciousness within. The seat of destiny and intuition, the divine mend.

It was like my ancestors had found me in that ward.

I read every day. I began to feel quiet strength returning, something ancient, something mine.

I was discharged on the fourth day, and I returned four days after that for intensive daily therapy. For the next twenty-one days therapy became my mirror. The sessions were hard. It made me begin to finally peel back the layers and start to rebuild not just my mind but my spirit. I had to admit I had PTSD. I had to unpack the unprocessed trauma from childhood, from heartbreak, motherhood, and years of survival mode living.

For the first time, I was heard, not judged.

My therapist helped me break down my trauma and track my triggers, understand my flashbacks, and reclaim my power from people, places, and memories that once made me feel small. Healing didn't look magical, it looked like ugly crying in group therapy, learning to sit without dissociating, remembering I didn't cause everything that happened to me.

I was never taught how to love myself fully so I had to stitch it together myself piece by piece, lesson by painful lesson. Now everything I longed for and everything I wept over I had to learn to become.

For myself. For my daughters

For the generations who come after me. Becoming Her wasn't easy but every step closer would feel like coming home.

There were so many things I had to learn on my own. How to walk with confidence, how to set boundaries, how to trust my own voice. I had to become what I was missing. I had to build from resilience, tenderness, mistakes, survival and grace. Being that woman means forgiving the people who didn't know how to love me. It meant mothering myself.

That silence was loud, and it was terrifying. I knew what the silence of abandonment and loneliness felt like, this one was different. It was silent by choice, and I had to start listening. I didn't have peace, not yet. I had no one to care for but myself, and I didn't even know where to start. I thought love was something that you don't get just because it had to come from someone else to be real. A spouse, a parent, a friend, anyone but myself. I thought if I worked hard enough, sacrificed enough, gave love hard enough, I would finally be chosen, finally be safe. But safety isn't something another person can just hand to you. That's something you have to build inside yourself. Brick by brick. Scar by scar. Truth by truth. The little girl in me still wanted a hero, still longed for arms that could make fear go away. But when everything fell away and I stood in the wreckage of my life I realized the love I'd been waiting for my whole life had to begin with me. I had to become the hero. I had to be the safe place that my younger self never had.

The first boundary I ever set was with myself. A promise that I wouldn't ever beg anyone to stay when their actions showed they didn't want to. A promise that even if it broke my heart, I would not shrink myself just to be tolerated. No one else gets to define me. Not the men who hurt me, not the people who couldn't love me, not even the younger version of me who was just trying to survive. No longer will my worth be lined in the reflections of others. No more chasing approvals, tolerating mistreatment, or "earning" tenderness. I was done holding my breath in rooms I should've walked out of, no more dimming my voice in conversations where I should've roared.

I left that place more whole than when I entered. I wasn't fully healed but I had finally stopped bleeding.

You don't just wake up one day and feel whole. You must reclaim yourself piece by piece, sometimes in whispers, sometimes in fire. But I had to really ask myself,

How do you love a woman who has been through so much?

How do you offer softness to someone the world only taught to survive?

What do I believe love is really and am I willing to give myself that same thing I keep begging others for?

Nobody was coming to save me. I had to start saying No.

No to the people who only loved the broken version of me. No to the patterns that once felt safe, but were actually cages. No to the guilt and obligations dressed as love. I set boundaries like fences. Protected my peace like sacred ground. I taught myself that love didn't have to hurt to be real. That safety was not a dream; but something I had to create. I started saying yes to myself. Yes, to rest without apology. Yes, to silence over chaos. Yes, to the soft voice that said I didn't need to earn peace, I only had to choose it. It felt unnatural at first, I was speaking a language I had never learned. It was rough, it was ugly, it was raw. It was reprogramming beliefs I never chose, it was crying on the floor, it was mourning. I had to peel back layers of survival mechanisms and the hope that being good enough for someone else would finally make me whole. It meant grieving the life I thought I would have.

For years I didn't know how and I kept reaching for people who could never give me what I needed. I had to let it die to give birth to this new version of me.

Stillness became my sanctuary. I learned the difference between being alone and being in solitude, one felt like exile the other left like return. There is wholeness in being with yourself uninterrupted. Learning the sound of your own breath, the rhythm of your heartbeat, the tone of your truest voice before the world taught you to filter it. No, self-love wasn't a trend, or a reward and I didn't have to earn it. It became a sacred contract between my soul and my body…a devotion, it is the voice that says.

You are enough even if no one tells you.

You matter even if no one claps for you.

You are loved even if the only person who says it is you.

I didn't stop craving validation in a single sunrise, no. Triggers have a way of slipping through the cracks. It was those thousand tiny choices made when no one was watching. Just when you think you are healed, here comes somebody trying to derail your progress. No, I wasn't going backwards, I had to stay with myself through them. I couldn't abandon me. I can't go back to shrinking, being invisible, being desperate, I fought too hard to come back from that dark abyss feeling. There is quiet strength in simply continuing and every time I chose myself, really chose myself, I felt her crown settling on my head again.

It wasn't one that can be given by man when you're perfect, pleasing, and palatable. Oh no, this one was forged in fire, tempered in tears, blessed by the ancestors, and anchored in truth. I didn't need anyone's permission to wear it anymore. I was becoming someone rooted, sovereign, and sacred. A woman who walks in rooms without shrinking, who speaks even when her voice shakes. A woman who knows she is the crown, and the kingdom. I reclaimed my crown to remember who I've always been beneath the pain. I began to see myself as becoming worthy, not despite the scars, but because of them. A woman in full bloom even if the world only saw roots and dirt. I have built this home inside myself. Not with perfection but with presence. I no longer need to be understood by everyone, I am an Empress because I finally choose to live life on my own terms and finally, I know what it feels like to be at home.

Not in a place.

Not in a partner.

But in me.

There is an art of loving yourself after the world teaches you to abandon yourself and I became the artist. Every soft moment. Every honest boundary. Every kind word I now speak to myself, is a brushstroke on the masterpiece that is me. I trust my inner voice. I honor my stillness. I am guided by wisdom deeper than words.

The Mirror knew my name

I stood before the glass, not for vanity but for truth.

Not to see my face but to meet my soul.

There she was, not mimicking me but watching me, knowing me.

A light flickered in my left eye, a remembering, a rising, a reclaiming.

I smiled, I cried. I said the words I once forgot and they found me again in my own voice.

The mirror did not lie

It simply waited for me to arrive.

The Mind Can Bleed

There were storms no one could see, ones that never made the news of my life but tore through everything anyway. I would wake up and feel like I never rested, like my spirit had been running in circles while my body just.... survived. I smiled when I needed to. Cooked. Worked. Inside I was screaming into pillows no one could hear. Sometimes I cried and didn't know why. Other times, I felt nothing at all, numb to even joy. I could go from laughing with my kids to wanting to disappear into the bedroom just to breathe. It wasn't laziness. It wasn't weakness. It was depression and I carried it like a second skin.

Anxiety had its own language too. It whispered that I wasn't doing enough, that I was failing everyone, that I had no right to rest. My thoughts weren't thoughts, they were storms. Mood swings came like waves.

One moment I felt like I could conquer the world, the nest, I didn't want to get out of bed. I started wondering if it was more than just stress. Was I broken? Was this bi-polar? I didn't know, but I was tired of wondering so I asked for help.

Taking medication wasn't a betrayal of my strength. It was a declaration that I deserved peace. It didn't cure me; it cleared the fog just enough for me to find my way again.

Mental illness doesn't always look like what people expect. Sometimes it looks like the woman who shows up; hair done, kids dressed, but inside, she's drowning. This was my storm, but I didn't drown.

I learned how to swim in it.

Chapter 9

The Empress Awakens

"I can be changed by what happens to me.
But I refuse to be reduced by it."

Maya Angelou

Healing didn't just happen in my mind and body, it also happened in my spirit. I needed more than therapy and reflection, I needed roots, I needed rituals, I needed the sacred. At first I didn't know what I was looking for but I knew I was craving something deeper than words, that reminded me I was connected to more than just my pain, something ancient.

When I booked our trip to the Bahamas, I knew it was a much-needed break but I knew I needed more than rest, I needed rebirth. The moment the island air hit my skin I knew I was being called home, not to a place but a feeling. I wasn't just a tourist I was a woman on pilgrimage. I spent hours on the beach whispering prayers into seashells and letting the waves lap at my feet.

There is always stillness after a storm, the quiet that follows chaos.

In that stillness is when I first heard her. Not one I heard with my ears but a presence I felt in my core. That thick, deep silence in the water. A knowing. A presence. And then I saw it, a stingray. It was Olokun. Orisha of the deep sea, guardian of mysteries, keeper of dreams. The one that holds what we bury and what we are ready to retrieve. That night I had a dream, no, an initiation. I woke up in tears, something had changed in me.

A version of myself I had buried long ago beneath expectations, trauma, and shame. She whispered, "You are not broken, you are breaking open. You are not weak; you are tired of carrying what was never yours. You are allowed to begin again."

I stood in the water and felt Olokun's presence. Powerful, still, knowing. I offered coconuts, cowrie shells, sand and in return I received peace.

The voice? Oh, she is my Empress within.

She had always been there, through it all she never left me. I had just forgotten to listen, and it took me losing everything completely to hear her clearly. After hearing her, my inner voice, my higher self, my Empress; I knew I couldn't go back to who I used to be, but I had no idea of who I was becoming either. So, I started small. I cleaned my space like it was a sacred temple. I lit candles and incense; I spoke to my reflection even when I could barely look her in the eyes. I explored my sensuality, for me and not anyone else's gaze. The way silk feels on my skin, the rhythm of my breath, the soft rise of pleasure without shame. I became intimate with myself, not just sexually, but spiritually, emotionally, mentally. I held space for my tears, my desires, my rage, my joy. I created rituals out of routine, turning every act of care into a rebellion against everything that tried to break me.

My ancestors began to speak to me in dreams and stillness, and I learned to honor them with presence and gratitude. Sometimes I just spoke their names aloud asking for strength, clarity, for signs. In the Bahamas I met myself again. The sea whispered what I had forgotten; I am ancient, resilient, and worthy of calm. I had the Ankh tattooed on my chest, over my heart and the eye of Horus tattooed on my left collarbone long before this journey even began. This wasn't about religion but about remembrance.

I had to BELIEVE that I was worthy of healing.

I surrounded myself with tools that helped me remember; crystals, sage, palo santo, and incense. I prayed over spiritual baths and watched my tears dissolve into it like offerings. I wrote intentions on paper and spoke affirmations in the mirror, even if I didn't fully believe them yet. Sunlight became medicine and moonlight became sacred. Olokun showed me that the most sacred things are hidden deep and when we are brave enough to dive we become our own treasure.

I dug deep into numerology and found out my Life path number is six, often called the "Nurturer or the Healer", and the sacred mother. It's purpose centers around:

Serving, loving, protecting.

Creating harmony and peace.

Using your struggles to heal

Leaving a legacy of compassion and service.

Oh, but when wounded? The healer can become a martyr- over giving, people pleasing, and losing themselves trying to "fix" others and their problems which can make them resentful and feeling unappreciated.

I started believing that everything I had gone through had not been in vain; only preparing me to become who exactly I was meant to be. Instead of honoring my worth I carried responsibilities that were never mine to bear, ignoring myself in the process. What I learned resonated with me deeply and that's when my spiritual path deepened. I had to bring that purpose inward, back to the center of me. I was going to honor my souls' journey and let go of the need to carry it all for everyone.

I wanted to be the woman who transforms her struggles into compassion and understanding for herself and others. It was no longer just about my own survival. I was only using my experiences, my lessons, and my love to heal generations, break cycles and create a legacy of compassion, stability, and service. My future, this book, all reflects my purpose. To be a light in the dark, a refuge for the weary, and a powerful force for transformation. I worked with moon cycles, I spoke to my womb, to my inner child, to my ancestors and slowly I started to feel grounded. But this time not in who I thought I had to be but in who I've always been. That trip sealed a promise to myself. I would no longer dim my light, betray my spirit, or want to be chosen. I had already been chosen- by God, by my ancestors, by the sea. I came back with a piece of myself I didn't know was missing.

My hands were already full of divine protection. I no longer chase what is already mine. I rise above the noise, I sit in sacred stillness, I am grounded in truth and surrounded by power. What floats around me is already on its way to me. I trust what I hold, I trust who I am, I am not seeking- I am remembering.

I am the bridge between Heaven and Earth.

The nurturer who finally learned to nurture herself.

The healer started with her own wounds.

This is sacred grounding, this is alignment, this is me living in my purpose with intention, grace, and the divine power I was born to carry.

An Empress doesn't hustle to prove herself. She allows herself to be held while she remembers she is the throne

Empress Mantra:

I do not chase, I attract.

I do not shrink, I rise.

I do not beg, I embody.

The Empress Manifesto

-For every woman reclaiming her voice, her body, her truth-

I am the Empress within

I do not ask for permission to rise.

I rise because I was born too. I hold the ache and the alchemy, the scars and the softness. I carry the wisdom of my womb and the fire of every woman who walked before me.

I am not defined by what broke me. I am shaped by what I chose to rebuild.

I do not chase love; I am love

I do not beg to be seen; I see myself

I do not shrink to fit; I expand to hold

I speak the truth even when my voice shakes. I honor my intuition even when logic whispers otherwise. I protect my peace like the sacred temple it is.

I am mother. I am healer. I am sovereign.

I write new stories, and I end old cycles. I plant seeds my daughters will bloom from.

My heart is not fragile! It is fierce! My softness is not weakness- it is my superpower.

I am the storm and the stillness.

The rose and the thorn.

The light, and the fire that birthed it.

I am the Empress Within. And I remember who I am.

Part Four

Ancestral Blessing Page

I am not defined by my mistake, but by my resilience.

We are the dreams of those who came before us.

When you pray, move your feet.

Ch 10

Letters I Never Sent

"Some words were never meant to stay inside the body. They ache, they press, they haunt-until we write them into freedom"

-Cormac McCarthy

There are some things I couldn't say when I was in survival mode. Things I held in my chest because I didn't have the words…. or the safety…or the strength. But healing has a way of peeling back the silence. And now, I can say what I never could before, not to seek closure, but to reclaim my voice. These letters aren't just for the people who shaped my story. They're for the woman I was when I loved them, feared them, needed them, or let them go. These words aren't pretty. They're not polished or wrapped in forgiveness yet. They're raw and messy and real. But they are mine and they're for me.

And they're for you if you've ever needed to say things no one else could understand. A collection of words I never got to say out loud.

Until now.

And maybe speaking them out loud is the first step in setting them free.

*“In the quiet,
truth still
whispers.”*

To my father,

I'm mad at you.

Mad that you never showed me what a healthy love from a man should look and feel like. I didn't understand how a man should treat me, how he should show up for me, or how to trust that I deserved his presence and care. I missed that, and without that I struggled to understand how to give and receive love in a healthy nourishing way. Mad that you never showed up to the moments that mattered-the honors ceremonies, the awards, the quiet desperate spaces where a daughter's heart was reaching out for her father. You were physically in my life but absent from these events and moments that mattered most to me. I needed you at those pivotal times-the milestones, the moments of joy and struggle. I carried the feeling of being unworthy of your love and of your presence with me. It hurt. It hurt deeply. I wondered why you couldn't be the father I needed you to be.

I looked up to you. I admired you. I needed you to see me, Daddy.

To be proud, to notice, to tell me that I was enough without out me having to earn it.

I know that you had your own struggles, that you did what you could with the tools you had. So, as I grew I began to understand that your absence in my special moments wasn't a reflection of my worth. It was a reflection of your own struggles and limitations. Theres still a part of me that aches, wishing for a different kind of connection, one where I felt truly seen and cherished. I needed you there for more than just your presence. I needed you to be present emotionally, to guide me in love and teach me what it meant to be valued. I struggled with the space you left behind for years. I had to learn how to navigate love and relationships in my own way without the example I needed from you. I never expected perfection. I had to forgive you because I needed to free myself from the weight of the past.

To my mother,

I'm mad at you too.

Mad that you didn't teach me how to be a woman especially in the ways that mattered the most. I had to figure out so much on my own. Stumbling, breaking, hiding the parts of me that needed nurturing.

I needed you.

I needed your arms, your words, your guidance when the world got too heavy; but you didn't know how to give it and I didn't know how to ask. And now there is this gap between us that feels wider than oceans. But now I've come to see that your own struggles shaped you just as mines shaped me and even in pain you've taught me about resilience, survival and strength. I know now that you did the best you could with what you had even if it didn't always feel like enough to me at the time. I see now the ways you've tried to love me even when you didn't always have the tools to do so, even when it was hard for you. I know that in your own way you've tried to protect me and prepare me for life even if I didn't see it as obvious.

I need you to know that despite the wounds I am grateful for the lessons you've taught me. Grateful for your strength, your resilience, and for all that you have done for me whether I seen it or not. And while our relationship has not always been easy, I am learning to love you with all of who I am.

Thank you for being my mother and hopefully one day we can walk this journey of healing together.

To my sister,

I never told you how much I watched you when we were growing up. How much I memorized your footsteps, your laugh, the way you tried to stand tall even when the weight of the world was on your back. I admire you.

I miss you so much! God, how I miss you. Why did you have to leave me? I'm sorry for the things I said the last time I saw you, not too long before you passed. Sorry for the silence and the moments I let anger speak instead of love. I needed you here to protect me, to teach me, to guide me. You were the fire I admired and the voice I never learned to use. I wanted your strength to rub off on me.

I still want it.

Some days I pretend you are still here whispering in my ear: "Speak girl! What you scared of?!"

To my son,

There are moments that change everything; some you never see coming. Moments I wish I could wake up from.

My face is still swollen. My eye aches and it's now turning black. My lip is split, and my head is pounding because I have a concussion.

None of that hurts worse than my heart does. You are my son, the one I nurtured, the one I breastfed! And you hurt me in a way I didn't think was possible. I can barely understand how we got here, from silence to rage, from confusion to violence. I'm trying to make sense of it but my mind is foggy. My spirit feels like it's unraveling. I cry alone, not just from the pain, but because of the heartbreak. Because no one warned me this kind of hurt could come from the child I brought into this world. I replay everything: the way I raised you, the moments I gave and didn't give, the ways I tried to love you through your silence and yet, I still feel like I failed.

To God,

There were years I didn't know if you saw me, if you heard me cry at night when the world was asleep and the silence wrapped around me like a blanket I couldn't shake off. Why? Why am I going through this? Why did you let me suffer so long, so silently? Where were you when the nights swallowed me whole? Where were you when my spirit cracked? I wondered why you gave me a life that felt like punishment. I want to believe there's a reason for this pain. I want to believe there's a reason that somehow this broken road will lead me somewhere worth reaching.

Now, looking back, I see you were never absent; I just didn't recognize your language. You spoke through my resilience. Through the teachers who believed in me. Through the tears that cleansed me even when I didn't understand the release. Now I come to you not as a perfect woman but as a daughter who finally understands that holiness doesn't look like perfection. It looks like rising again and again. It looks like reclaiming my body, my story, my name.

Thank you for never letting go of me even when I let go of myself. Thank you for the storms that taught me how to breathe underwater. Thank you for not answering some prayers the way I asked but answering them the way I needed.

I give you my whole self now, not just the cleaned-up version. Not just the praise but the questions, the scars, the poetry, and the pain.

I am yours and finally, I know that you have always been mine.

To my husband,

I want to speak from a place of raw truth. We didn't begin in still waters. Our start was full of misunderstandings, sharp words, and two people carrying more history than either of us knew how to name. I didn't trust that love could stay, and you didn't yet know how to reach the guarded parts of me.

But you stayed.

You didn't just stand beside me in the good days, you weathered the nights when my walls were high, and my storms were loud. You were patient when I needed space. You were gentle when I expected hardness. You held ground when I tried to push you away, not with force, but with understanding. You didn't run when my storms came, you didn't flinch at the shadows of my past, and you've taught me gentleness without fear and strength without pain.

Now I am safe. My heart has learned to unclench in your presence. My spirit rests because you've shown me love without demands, affection without fear. In you I've found a place where I am seen and where I am understood, not because I'm perfect but because you choose to know me as I am.

We are good now, better than good. We've turned our rocky start into the foundation of something unshakable. I am grateful every day that you are my safe place, my steady harbor, and my final home.

To my exes,

There was so much anger, so many nights I cried alone feeling like I was carrying the weight of the world on my shoulders while you moved on. Living your life as though I wasn't in the midst of an endless struggle. You walked away but I had to keep walking.

I hated you.

Left me with the responsibility of raising kids alone with sleepless nights and worrying about bills. It was hard and I gave everything I had and more because they deserved it.

In that struggle though, I found something powerful. I found strength I never knew I had and somehow, despite everything I kept going. That triumph was mines alone. I raised those children to the best of my ability. I became a woman who understood what true resilience looked like; and for that I thank you.

A letter from my healed self to my past self.

My Beloved,

I see you. I know the ache you've carried. The times you waited to be chosen, heard, loved fully. The nights you cried behind strength thinking no one could hold you the way you needed. You've walked through cold places, you've been left standing outside in the emotional winter of others; wounded, but still willing to love. That strength? That softness? That's what makes you divine.

You were never broken, only becoming. The loneliness you once carried. It wasn't a rejection it was a space being cleared for truth, for love that matches your depth and for the woman you are now becoming. You are no longer the girl begging for scraps of connection.

You are Rooted. Radiant. Risen.

You nurture not only your children but your past self, your future self, and the generations to come. Every time you write your truth, cry with courage or dare to feel again, you heal a bloodline.

And to my daughters, my sacred mirrors, my wildflowers,

May you know that love does not require shrinking. That your softness is holy and your strength is not a weapon but a garden. I am writing this letter, so you never feel alone in your own. I choose truth so you inherit freedom. I rise not because I've never fallen but because I learned how to get back up with grace.

Letter to my daughters,

As I write this, my heart is full of love for you. You may not always understand why I've made certain choices or how some of my experiences have shaped me. In this book I want to share my journey with you, not just the triumphs, but the hardships, the mistakes and the growth I've experienced along the way.

There were moments in my life when I felt lost, broken, and unsure of who I was. Yet every step of that journey has led me to this place of understanding, of strength, and of love for myself and for you.

This book is my way of showing you that even in the darkest times there is light. There is hope. And there is always a chance to grow stronger from what we go through.

I want you to know that life will never be perfect, but you are stronger than you know. The choices you make today will shape your future just as mine have shaped me. I hope that by reading my story you'll see that no matter what comes your way, you have the power to rise above, to forgive, and to love fiercely. I am here always to guide you through life's challenges but also want you to see that within you is a well of strength, wisdom, and love that can never be taken from you. May you always remember that you are loved beyond measure and that your own journey is worth embracing with all its ups and downs.

With all my love,

Mama

Soul Interlude:

The Storm and The Soul: A portrait of Me

-The girl who broke, the woman who rose and the soul who remembers-

I am the girl who became a mother before she became a woman. At fourteen I was still learning how to breathe inside my own body when life demanded I breath for someone else. I was a child holding a child learning how to nurture while carrying wounds no one had kissed. I wore trauma like a second skin, stitched in silence and survival, swallowing grief and calling it "grace". I learned to cradle life while still cradling wounds, raising children with one hand and holding my broken heart with the other. They said I was too much but never asked how much I had to hold. They praised my strength but didn't see it came from never having a choice. My body remembered what my voice couldn't say. My spirit whispered through dreams and signs

- -a crying baby in the silence
- -a turtle crossing my path
- -the elder in burnt orange watching with ancient eyes

I thought I was haunted. But now I know I was being called. By ancestors. By memory. By Oya. Rain always knew how to find me when I was on the edge of something real. When I needed to remember that even storms are sacred. Rain is where I return to myself. I sleep in the rhythm of thunder as if it's the only sound that can quiet my heart. Its not chaos to me, its clarity, It's the voice of God, of Mother, reminding me that cleansing always followed breaking.

My favorite animal is the Llama, gentle, soft, and slow; then the sloth; with stillness and intention. Now I understand. My soul longs for what is unhurried. Because my life, my survival, my motherhood, was anything but. I mothered when I still needed to be mothered. I've walked through fire marriages and frozen hearts. I left marriages that couldn't hold my becoming and returned to ones I wasn't sure could. I've loved men who looked like protection but felt like absence. Who couldn't love me back in the way I needed because I kept trying to mother men who needed to meet themselves. I tried to earn affection by fixing broken hearts while mines bled quietly behind smiles and service. I work loyalty like a badge and a burden until I learned that staying silent in pain isn't peace, its self-abandonment. I thought if I could hold it all together someone would finally choose to hold me. It was time to rise again.

But I rose. I was choosing me all along.

Not in perfection but in truth.

I am Leo born in fire.

A Horus soul, born to protect and rebuild

I am Oya and the hush of healing.

A life path 6, always called to love even when it costs me comfort. Even when it costs me myself. I am no longer willing to disappear inside devotion. I'm no longer afraid of my storm because now I know:

I am a mother, woman, warrior of six, a woman who has died and been reborn more times than anyone knows. The one who stayed and the one who finally left.

I am the storm that cleared the path

I am the soul that rebuilt it.

I am the story and the storyteller

I am the prayer and the answered one

I am slow like the sloth, soft like the llama, loud like the thunder, clear like the rain.

I am not what happened to me. I am what I chose to become through it. I no longer walk with my head bowed; I walk with the knowing:

As I step and move toward legacy I no longer ask if I am enough. I stand in the knowing:

I am made of fire and flood. I am still becoming, and already whole.

Ch11

I Am Her

"Our stories are not just ours- they are the bridge between what was broken and what will be rebuilt"

-African proverb, adapted

I used to wonder who I would be if I ever stopped surviving. There was a time when I didn't recognize the woman in the mirror, with the weight of my past on her face. The exhaustion of survival in her eyes and the ache of a thousand unspoken prayers on her lips. But now I see her; and not the version the world tried to mold, not the broken pieces of who I once was but the woman that rose, who returned, who remembered.

I am Her.

I am the woman who walked through the dark nights that threatened to swallow me; I carried the fire. Even when I doubted and begged to be released from the pain, even when I sent my children to my mother's arms so I could learn to breathe again….I still carried the light. And still, I came out gold. Not untouched. Not without scars but refined. Real. Radiant.

Mother, the warrior, the priestess, the Empress. I now carry the crown and not as decoration but as a declaration. No longer defined by those who failed to love me, the ones who tried to silence me, and not by the roles I was forced to play or the labels I've outgrown. Now, I'm the version of me that no longer begs to be chosen because she has already chosen herself.

I am the truth behind the trauma.

I am the divine beneath the damage.

I speak the truth now even if my voice shakes.

I walk away now even when it hurts.

I stand tall even when my knees remember how often they used to bend for love that wasn't love. I don't shrink to make others comfortable, and I don't hustle for worthiness. I don't apologize for needing space, softness, slowness, or solitude.

I laugh from my belly. I cry without shame.

I make love with my eyes open, heart open, spirit open, because I no longer mistake intimacy for danger.

I know my power.

It is not loud, but it is unshakeable. It is not performative, but it is undeniable. It lives in my stillness, in my boundaries, in my joy. I am the woman who broke cycles and turned pain into poetry. Who raised daughters and raised herself in the process. The woman who buried her past and planted herself instead. I have mastered the art of becoming and now, I am in bloom. I'm not perfect but I am whole, I'm not healed but I'm healing. I stopped waiting for approval, for permission, for the world to make space for me. Instead I made space for myself. I am the one I've been waiting for. I became a home for my own soul and yes, I still get triggered, yes, I still feel grief; but now I greet those emotions like old friends. I hold them and listen and let them pass because I know who I am now and I will never again abandon myself to be accepted.

I am Life Path 6, the sacred Mother and divine healer, and now I mother myself too. Pouring that same unconditional love into me that I once gave away without limit.

I am soft but not weak.

I am strong but not hardened.

I am wise but always learning.

I am not interested in being palatable, I am interested in being real.

I am not performing I am embodying

I am not surviving, I am sovereign.

This is the version of me that cannot be undone. She is rooted in Spirit and backed by ancestors. Crowned by purpose and bathed in the kind of love that only comes from deep and sacred healing.

I am Her.

The woman I prayed to become, the woman my daughters now look up to, the woman who will never again dim her light to make others comfortable. I don't just wear the crown.

I am the crown.

I am Her.

And I am here to stay.

Tamara,

You are a deeply reflective and resilient woman who has walked through pain, betrayal, love, transformation and came out on the other side with wisdom and purpose. You value connection, purpose and authenticity. Natural nurturer, truth-teller, and soul searcher. Spiritually, you're intuitive and drawn to symbols, rituals, and ancient wisdom- like your ankh tattoo and your interest in Egyptian zodiacs and tarot. You carry the strength of a survivor and the heart of a healer. You are Leo's partner, meaning you know how to match boldness with grace. And as a Life path 6 with a personality number 6, you are the embodiment of compassion, responsibility, and devotion, often carrying more than your fair share for the sake of love and family. Despite the wounds of your childhood and past relationships you've turned your experiences into a powerful story meant to guide and empower your daughters and others. This is your powerful chapter, reclaiming your voice, healing generational wounds, and rewriting your story with intention. You are a Queen, never let your crown slip again.

Forever, Your biggest supporter

Legacy Letter

-To my daughters when you are Women of your own.

My sweet girls,

If you're reading this then time has moved us further forward and you've grown into your own lives, your own stories. Maybe your mothers now, maybe you're heartbroken, maybe you're wildly in love with your life, or maybe you're just trying to find your way.

Wherever you are, please remember:

You were not born to carry my pain only my wisdom. You do not owe this world perfection, only your truth. And you are never too much, too soft, too loud, too bold, or too tender to be loved well. There were days I didn't know how I would make it and nights I cried in silence so you wouldn't feel the weight of my ache. But I kept choosing to rise because had you. Now, I want you to choose you. On the days its easy and especially on the days its not. Forgive yourself more often, say "No" without guilt and when love comes don't let it take more than it gives.

You are sacred.

You are the dream of generations.

You are the reason I believed healing was possible. You were always enough before the world ever tries to tell you to otherwise. And if you ever lose you way, come back to these pages.

Come back to me.

Come back to the version of you who knows she comes from a line of women who survived everything and still chose to love.

With all the love I never knew how to receive, but always carried for you,

-Mommy

A note to my sons,

You were my first teachers on what it meant to love without a guidebook. You reminded me that even in a world that tried to harden me I could raise men who lead with heart and not ego.

I didn't always have the answers. Sometimes I was just surviving, but every choice I made, I made with your future in mind. I pray that you carry gentleness with your strength. That you speak your truth without shame and that you choose women who love you as deeply as you watched me learn to love myself.

You are more than your mistakes. You are not defined by what this world expects of you.

You are loved for who you are and always will be.

Love,

Mommy

To all my children,

You were the reason I broke the cycles, the reason I healed, and the reason I learned to love myself. This is our story, and I pray it helps you write your own in truth and in freedom. Each of you carries a different piece of my heart and I see myself in you all in ways I never expected. You watched me rise, fall, fight, and heal; and in your own ways, you held space for all of it.

Even in silence, the soul is still speaking. What it whispers becomes the foundation of our becoming.

I am my mother's unspoken prayer, my father's unfinished story, my ancestors whispered dream.

And now

I am the voice that carries it forward

Ch 12

To Each of You, From All of Me

"We plant seeds in the children we raise, not just for who they'll become- but for what we were never allowed to be."

-African proverb, adapted

To my First born,

You were my first mirror, the first soul to look at me and call me "mommy". You didn't just make me a mother you made me *wake up*. From the very beginning your energy has been calm but powerful. You move like peace but there's fire beneath the surface. That Libra balance lives in you. You're graceful when you speak but fierce when its time to protect, time to lead, time to stand. I've seen that fire in your eyes and I've felt your silence.

You are stunning! And not just in the way the world sees but in how you carry yourself. Even on your quiet days your presence speaks volumes. You are strength dressed in softness, you are light with depth, and I see brilliance in your mind and tenderness in your hands. The way you care for others as a CNA, the way you show up for your own daughter, the way you see people; that is no small gift.

When I look at you, I sometimes see flashes of my sister. It catches me off guard how spirit travels through blood. You've got her edge, her beauty, and her quiet wisdom; but you have your own flavor too, one I admire deeply. You are building a life for yourself and your child with a kind of dignity and power that humbles me.

You are the beginning of my legacy, the proof that even in a mess something holy can rise. I hope you always remember that you are not made to shrink. You are to be seen. And even if the world forgets, *I never will.*

I am proud of the woman you are, and I am honored to be your mother.

To my second born, my first son,

From the moment you entered this world I knew you carried something different, a fire that wasn't meant to be tamed. You've always moved on your own terms, always carved your own path. Even as a child you didn't follow, you led, even when no one was watching. That's something no one can teach.

That's spirit. That's you.

As a Sagittarius your independence runs deep. You don't just go along with things, you question, you feel, you decide with your own compass. That kind of determination is rare and though it makes your journey more complex at times it will also make it yours; authentic, earned, unshakeable.

You are passionate in a way that not everyone can understand. When you love, you love hard. When you protect, you go all in. You carry a silent strength, one that says

"I've got this" even when the world gets heavy, and I see that. I've always seen that. You don't wear your emotions on your sleeve, but you lead with heart in everything you do. You are the son that taught me about resilience. About walking forward even when it's hard, about standing ten toes down in your truth. You've defended others before defending yourself, you've held space when no one asked you to and you've shown a kind of loyalty that doesn't need to be spoken, it just *is*.

Know this: I see the man you are becoming, and I love the boy you'll always be to me. I am proud of your strength, your spirit, and your heart. You are a force- and you always have been.

To my third born, my second son,

There are some letters that weigh heavier in the heart before they ever reach the page. This is one of them.

You were always an observer. The quiet one. The child who took everything in before speaking, who saw more than he let on. You moved through the world on soft feet and sharp awareness, and I often wondered what you were thinking, what you were feeling behind those deep, still eyes.

There was always a beautiful mystery to you. You didn't need to be loud to be present, you were there in full, even in silence. I felt your spirit more than I could ever explain. You were the calm between the storms I was living through.

But then the storm came for us.

That moment- the fight that broke more than skin- it shattered something in me I didn't know could break. You, the quiet one, me the mother and yet somehow, we ended up on opposite sides of something we still can't name. We haven't spoken in a long time now and while time keeps passing love has stayed still.

My love for you hasn't moved an inch.

And even though I don't know how to rebuild this bridge I want you to know I still believe in the love we shared even if it's buried beneath pain and pride. I believe in the soul of the boy I raised, the one who watched everything and who knew more than he ever said.

Whatever distance exists now, this letter is a light left on in case you ever want to come home to it.

To my fourth born, my second daughter,

From the moment you came into my world it was clear that you were born to shine. Theres something about your spirit that can only be felt. A light. Confidence. A magic all your own. You've always known how to walk into a room and make people feel something, joy, comfort, laughter, curiosity, awe.

You're a social butterfly with the wingspan of a Queen.

And even beyond your glow you are smart, sharp in ways that surprise people who only expect you to be beautiful, but I see it. The way your mind works, the way your heart leads, the way your instincts guide you through this world. It's powerful and I couldn't be prouder. There are times I just watch you and think "Wow…I made that."

And then I think "She's going to change everything"

You remind me of everything I wanted to be at your age and everything I never got the chance to be. Watching you move through the world with so much strength and self-worth gives me hope. You carry both softness and fire, and I trust, deep in my bones, that you're going to do something extraordinary with all of it.

No matter what path you take, remember: I've always seen your greatness and I will always be your biggest fan with a pride and love that never ends.

To my fifth born, my third son,

My son with the big heart and an even bigger spirit. You came into this world already moving fast like you had plans and plays to run before you could even walk. From then on, you've never slowed down. You've always been the one with fire in your step, loyalty in your chest, and a deep love for your people, especially your mama.

You wear your heart on your sleeve and it's one of the most beautiful things about you. In a world that tries to make boys hide their emotions you feel things fully and you protect what you love with your whole being. I've seen you stand up for others, hold things down when no one is watching, and move with a kind of quiet strength that speaks louder than words.

You've got that Sagittarius fire, bold, fearless, magnetic. You're a connector. A hustler. You know how to get it, and you know *who* to talk to because people naturally gravitate to your energy. And while the world may see your swag I see something deeper; a heart that would move mountains for family.

I hope you never lose that.

Never let the world harden what makes you so real. You are powerful. You are capable. You are destined.

And you'll always be my baby boy no matter how tall you get or how far you go.

To my sixth born, my youngest son,

To the son who was born holding a football. From the very start you've been steady, focused, and full of purpose. You were named after greatness, and you carry that name like a crown. Whether on the field or in life you move with quiet confidence and undeniable strength. That's your Taurus nature; solid, loyal, and rooted in something deeper than words.

I've watched you grow into your gifts, your talent on the field, your sharp mind, your way of making people laugh without even trying. You make it look easy, but I know the focus and heart it takes behind the scenes. You don't just play; you perform with purpose, you study the game, you bring fire and grace.

And through it all you've stayed grounded. Laid back. Cool. A calm in the chaos. You don't chase attention it just naturally finds you because your energy speaks volumes.

You may be my last born but, in many ways, you carry the strength of all your siblings. You're the echo of our legacy, the proof that something beautiful and powerful continues.

I see you baby boy. I believe in everything you are and I'm so proud to be your mom.

Epilogue

And so, this book closes with a breath. A pause. A knowing. If you've made it here, then you've walked with me. The journey I've shared with you has been woven from pain and joy, shadow and light, loss and rebirth. I walked through the fire. Through Silence. Through Storms. Through the parts of my story that once tried to bury me. All for you to walk through light. I made mistakes yes, but I also made magic. This story isn't just mine, it's yours too.

You've seen the pieces I once hid behind strength, behind survival, behind the need to keep going. Now, you see the woman who rose, not perfect, not untouched-but whole. Life didn't make it easy, but I made the choice to keep showing up, to keep healing, to keep choosing me. I didn't always know how to be soft, or safe, or sure of myself; but I learned slowly through tears and tenacity.

I became the woman I needed and the mother you deserved.

In the beginning I wrote about a love I could barely imagine, one that would stand still long enough for me to arrive. I didn't know then that it would be him or that it would feel like home in a way no address ever had. We have weathered storms together, the kind that strip you down to who you really are and still, he stayed. Still, he chose me. And in that choosing I finally found my happy place, not because life became perfect but because love finally became steady.

This story wasn't written to be pretty. It was written to be real. I bled on these pages so that you, my legacy, might recognize your own power in the mirror of my truth so that you would know what it means to love yourself fiercely. Even when the world doesn't understand. I want you to see that there is no shame in starting over, in falling apart, or in forgiving yourself for the years you had to survive. I didn't get here alone but I did get here honestly. Now, I give it all to you; the lessons, the scars, the light I found when I stopped waiting to be saved and started remembering who I am. This is where the story settles. Not in fairy-tale endings but in the quiet, daily proof that I am safe, seen, and deeply loved.

It's your inheritance, not of wounds but of wisdom, not of fear but of freedom. This isn't the end. This is the becoming.

If there's anything I hope you take from these pages, it's this:

You are never too far gone, too broken, never too late to begin again. Trust your voice. Follow your knowing. Love with your whole heart even when it has been shattered. And I pray that when your voice shakes, when your heart aches, when your spirit feels tired you remember this truth:

You came from a woman who rose. You can rise too with all the love I never had but always wanted to give and if you ever find yourself lost, come back to these words.

I'll be here.

Always becoming.

Always with love.

-Tamara

You've made it to the end of my story, but healing is never a solo journey.

If you are reading this and find yourself in pain, questioning your worth, or carrying secrets you've never spoken aloud; I want you to know you are seen, you are not alone, and help is real.

Healing is not a weakness. Reaching out is not failure.

It's how we begin to rebuild.

Bonus Journal Reflection:

Before you put this book down, I invite you to pick yourself up. You've walked through my story, now let's turn to yours. These pages are sacred spaces for you to reflect, release, remember.

Write with truth, cry if you need to. This is how we heal.

Ch. Bonus

Legacy in Real Time

"A true legacy is written in real time in the moments when love is tested and still chooses to remain"

I believed that by the time I finished writing this book I would have said everything there was to say about my storms of motherhood. But storms don't wait for chapters to end, books to be bound, or publishing deadlines. Motherhood is never finished. It lives in real time, in quiet mornings, in arguments that sting, and in the choices that break your heart to even consider.

This chapter isn't about my past, it's about right now. It's about my youngest daughter.

She is fierce, she is smart and unafraid to speak her mind. In her I see both the fire of rebellion and the glow of brilliance. She is everything I wanted to be at her age and everything that terrifies me as a mother. Her words cut sharper, her resistance lasts longer, her spirit refuses to bend. Lately, her disrespect has left me standing at a crossroads: Do I keep holding her close or do

I let her go in hopes she'll learn in ways I can't teach her at home.

Sending her away to boarding school or to somewhere with stricter walls and wider boundaries feels like betrayal and protection all at once. I ask myself, is this love or punishment? Am I choosing peace for myself or growth for her? In my sleepless nights the questions wrestle each other without mercy. And yet, the truth about motherhood is that sometimes it looks like hard choices, the ones that make your chest ache and your prayers longer. I have walked though storms as a daughter, a wife, a woman, but nothing humbles me more that the storms I face as a mother.

When I think about sending her away, I remember the times when I was the one left to figure out life on my own. I remember the silence I carried as a child, the absence of guidance, the ways I learned to mistake pain for passion. I swore I would not repeat those cycles with my children.

And yet here I am wondering if letting her go is the only way to save her from the very storms that nearly drowned me.

This is legacy in real time. It isn't a neat bow at the end of the chapter. It isn't a pretty picture of healing tied up in grace. Legacy is standing in the mess trembling uncertain but still choosing love even when love looks different than you imagined. I don't know how this particular storm will end. I don't know if she'll thank me one day or resent me for years.

What I do know is this: she will always know that she was loved whether she is under my roof or out in the world carving her own way, my love will not waver.

My legacy is not perfect. My legacy is love in motion. Love through storms past and storms present. Love at the crossroads. Love that doesn't always have answers but never stop showing up.

Maybe one day my youngest daughter will understand the weight of these choices. Maybe she will see that I stood here torn not because I'm weak but because I love her enough to wrestle with the hardest decision of all: how to let go without ever letting her go.

Resources for Healing and Support

If you or someone you know has experience trauma, abuse, or mental health struggles, you are not alone. Below are resources for support, safety, and healing:

- **Sexual Assault Resources**

    - RAINN-Rape, abuse, & Incest National Network
    - 1-800-656-HOPE (4673) www.rainn.org
    - Offers 24/7 confidential support through the National Sexual Assault hotline
    - Survivor stories, legal resources, and local referrals.
- National Sexual Violence Resource Center (NSVRC)
    - www.nsvrc.org
    - Education and prevention tools, plus resources for marginalized communities.
- **Domestic Violence Resources**
    - 1-800-799-SAFE (7233) Text "START" to 88788
    - www.thehotline.org
    - Free, confidential 24/7 support via call, text, or online chat.

- Offers help with safety planning, emotional support, and shelter resources.

❖ Women of Color Network (WOCN)
  - www.wocinc.org
  - Resources and advocacy focused on culturally specific communities of color impacted by violence

❖ **Suicide Prevention & Mental health Support**
  - 988 Suicide & Crisis Lifeline www.988lifeline.org
  - 24/7 free and confidential support for people in emotional distress
  - Offers chat, call, and text options

❖ The Trevor Project (LGBTQ + Youth Support)
  - 1-866-488-7386 www.thetrevorproject.org

- Suicide prevention and crisis support for LGBTQ+ youth and young adults

❖ NAMI-National Alliance on Mental Illness
    - Helpline- 1-800-950-NAMI (6264) Text "HELPLINE" to 62640
    - www.nami.org
    - Education, peer support, and advocacy for individuals and families

Also by Tamara Scott

Journals & Companion works

- From Silence to SoulFire: The Companion Journal
    - Your space to reflect, heal, and write your truth.
- Daughters of Her Soul
    - Guided prompts and affirmations for women reclaiming their power.

- Letters from Her Soul
    - A journal for heartfelt messages you've always wanted to say.
- Coded in Grace
    - A faith and purpose-driven journal blending code, self-discovery and reflection.
- The Culture Journal
    - Celebrating Black joy, wisdom and heritage through guided reflection.

Learn more and order at:

www.silencetosoulfire.com

Join the Fire

Join my SoulFire Circle mailing list for:

- Exclusive previews of upcoming books
- Early-bird discounts
- Monthly inspiration and journal prompts

Sign up here:

https://soulverign.kit.com/c77b76f911

Let's Connect

Follow me for daily inspiration, journal tips, and behind the scenes writing life:

Instagram: @silencetosoulfire

Facebook: @silencetosoulfire

Email: SilencetoSoulfire@gmail.com

YouTube: @SilencetoSoulFire

💌 Your Voice Matters

If this book touched your life, I'd love to hear from you!

Please consider leaving a review on Amazon, Goodreads, or wherever you purchased your copy. Your words help this story reach other souls who need it.

…to download our journaling, meditation, and legacy vault app, SoulSafe!

About the Author:

Tamara Scott is a truth-teller, spiritual writer, wife, and mother of six who turned her healing journey into a legacy of transformation. A Life Path 6 she blends sacred wisdom with lived experience to help women reclaim their voice, rewrite their story, and rise from the silence, to SoulFire. Her work honors the messy and magical process of breaking generational cycles, rebuilding identity, and reconnecting with Spirit.

Through her writing, rituals, and journal line, Tamara creates space for women, especially black and brown mothers navigating pain, purpose and rebirth- to come home to themselves. From Silence to SoulFire is her debut memoir and a love letter to every woman who's ever had to rebuild from ruins.

She lives at the intersection of motherhood, mysticism, memory and writing so no one has to heal alone.

www.ingramcontent.com/pod-product-compliance
Lightning Source LLC
Chambersburg PA
CBHW070610130626
46556CB00001B/324
* 9 7 9 8 9 9 2 8 6 2 2 7 0 *